Lonely

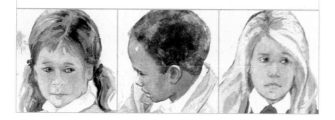

A CHERRYTREE BOOK

This edition first published in 2007
by Cherrytree Books, part of
The Evans Publishing Group Limited
2A Portman Mansions
Chiltern St
London
W1U 6NR

Printed in Malaysia

British Library Cataloguing in Publication Data

Amos, Janine
Lonely. - 2nd ed. - (Feelings)
1. Loneliness - Juvenile literature 2. Solitude - Juvenile literature
I. Title
155.9'2

ISBN 9781842344781
First published in paperback1997

CREDITS
Editor: Louise John
Designer: D. R. ink
Production: Jenny Mulvanny

Lonely

By Janine Amos
Illustrated by Gwen Green

CHERRYTREE BOOKS

Una's story

It was Joanne's birthday party. All the children were sitting quietly. They were watching Fiz Wiz the magician and her puppet Bonzo.

"You'll all have to help with this trick," said Bonzo. "It's a new one. I may need some more practice to get it just right. You can help me by wishing hard."

Everyone helped. Most of the children held hands and giggled with excitement. Una was sitting on her own. She didn't hold anyone's hand. But she was wishing just as hard as the others.

The trick worked! Bonzo pulled a bunch of flowers out of his hat. He took a bow and everyone clapped. It was the end of the show.

Una watched the other children run off to play. She started to follow them. But then she stopped.

"I can't join in," she thought. "I won't know what to say." She felt left out.

"Hello! Why aren't you playing with your friends?" asked Fiz Wiz. Una didn't answer.

Why won't Una answer Fiz Wiz?

Fiz Wiz had a lot of things to tidy away. There were three puppets, some masks and twenty coloured scarves. Una helped. She passed Fiz Wiz her magic wand and the paper flowers. Fiz Wiz put them into a big box. And all the time, Fiz Wiz talked to Una. She told her lots of silly jokes. But Una didn't say a word.

When they had finished, Fiz Wiz thanked Una for her help.
"I used to be shy, like you," said Fiz Wiz.
Una couldn't believe that!
"I'll tell you a secret," said Fiz Wiz quietly. "Bonzo has some magic especially for shy people."
As Una watched, Fiz Wiz wriggled her hand – and Bonzo came to life again.

What do you think the magic will be?

"I'll whisper," said Bonzo. Una leaned forward to listen. "The magic is to think about other people. Try to forget about yourself – just for a moment."

"But how do you start?" asked Una.

"You start with a question!" said Bonzo. "There's always one question you can ask."

"You're using the magic now," Fiz Wiz said.

"What do you mean?" asked Una.

"You're talking to me," said Fiz Wiz, "and it gets easier each time you do it!"

"Just like a magic trick!" laughed Una.

Just then, Joanne ran in from the garden. She was puffing and she looked happy. Una wondered what games the others were playing outside. She started to feel left out again.

If you were Una, what would you do now?

Just in time, Una remembered Bonzo's magic.

"Are you having a good time, Joanne?" she asked. "What are you playing?"

"Hide-and-seek!" said Joanne. "Come and play with us." Joanne took hold of Una's hand.

As Una ran off, she waved to Bonzo and Fiz Wiz.

"It works!" she called.

"Just like all my magic!" said Fiz Wiz.

How did Fiz Wiz help?
Who would you talk to if you felt shy?

Feeling like Una

Have you ever felt left out, like Una? Have you ever been too shy to join in? If you have, you'll know how lonely it makes you feel. You think you're the only one who isn't having a good time.

Don't let shyness win

Shyness can stop you doing the things you'd like to do. It can make you go red and feel afraid to speak. But try not to worry. Most people feel shy sometimes. Try to think about something else for a moment. Try to carry on with what you want to do. Don't let shyness win.

Helping yourself

You can try to find out more about other people. You can ask them questions about themselves. You can try to stop worrying about how you are feeling. It's hard at first – but practice helps.

Talking helps

Read the stories in this book. Think about the people in them. Do you feel like them sometimes? Next time you feel lonely, ask yourself some questions. What can I do to help myself? Who can I talk to? Then find someone you trust – a teacher or a parent. Tell them how you are feeling. Talking helps.

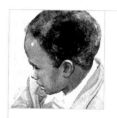

Calvin's story

Calvin was in his room. He gave his model plane a big push. It crashed into the cupboard. Calvin threw himself on to his bed. Bang! went the bed against the wall.

"Quiet!" shouted Calvin's big brother Josh. Josh was in the room next door, doing his homework.

Calvin looked around his room.

"What can I do?" he thought. "I've read all my books. I've made my bed. I'm tired of my puzzles. I'm bored, bored, bored!"

Calvin sighed. He put his hands in his pockets and went downstairs.

Calvin walked along the hall. He started to sing. Calvin had a special song for when he felt bored. There were no words and there wasn't much of a tune. He sang very loudly.

"Pom, Pom, Pom," went Calvin. He trailed through to the kitchen. "Pom, POM!"

"That's a terrible noise!" said Calvin's mum crossly. "You'll wake Ashley. Go outside and play."

Calvin sighed again. He walked down the path. As he went, Calvin kicked at the ground. He watched the toes of his shoes turning white. Scuff, scuff went Calvin's feet. "Pom, Pom," he sang.

Soon a head popped out from under the car.
"Stop that awful noise, Calvin!" said Dad.
Calvin gave a great, big sigh. He sat down near to the fence. He watched his dad fixing the car. Calvin found a stick and ran it along the fence. Crick! went the stick.

Calvin sat and thought about his friends at school. He wondered what they were all doing.

"I wish I didn't live so far away from the other boys," he thought, and all the time he ran the stick along the fence.

How is Calvin feeling?

"Calvin!" shouted his dad after a while. "Put that stick down and come over here." Calvin dropped the stick and went over to his dad.

"What's the matter with you?" asked Calvin's dad.

"Nothing," said Calvin. "Well, there's nothing anyone can do about it, anyway."

"There's always something you can do – about anything," said Calvin's dad. "What's the matter?"

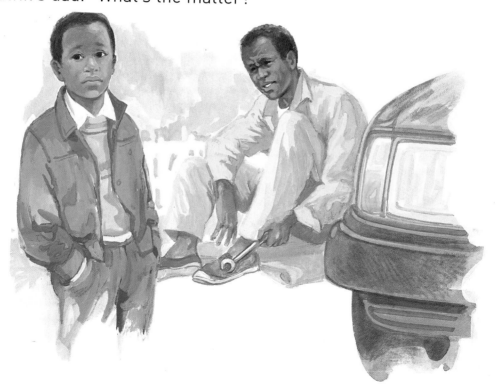

"I'm bored," said Calvin. "I can't play with Josh because he's too old – and Ashley's just a baby. The boys at school don't live near here. I'm bored."

"You sound lonely to me," said Calvin's dad.

Calvin's dad sat down on the path, next to Calvin.

"Let's think of some ways for you to make friends nearby," he said.

"They all know each other already," said Calvin quietly. "I don't count."

"It's no use just feeling sorry for yourself. You have to go out and make friends sometimes," said Calvin's dad.

Then Calvin's dad held up one hand.

"Five ways to stop feeling lonely!" he said. He counted them off on his fingers.

"One – join gym club. Two – join swimming club. Three – go to the drama group. Four – join choir. Five – invite a schoolfriend home for tea."

What do you think of Calvin's dad's ideas?
Can you think of anything else that Calvin could do?

Calvin's dad looked proud of himself.

"Which shall you do first?" he asked.

"Swimming club!" shouted Calvin. "And I'd like to have Bob over for tea on Saturday."

Calvin's dad jumped up.

"Get your coat, then," he said.

"Where are we going?" asked Calvin.

"To the sports centre – to sign you up for swimming club!" said Calvin's dad.

At teatime, Calvin couldn't stop grinning.

"I'm going to swimming club every Monday evening," he told his mum. "And is it all right to ask Bob over on Saturday?"

"That's fine," said Calvin's mum, laughing, "so long as you don't teach him to sing!"

How do you think Calvin feels now?

Feeling like Calvin

Sometimes it feels good to be on your own. There are all kinds of things that you can do by yourself, like reading, painting, making models, listening to music. But it's fun to share with others, too. Spending a lot of time by yourself can make you feel bored and lonely, like Calvin.

What can you do?

If you're feeling like Calvin, think what you can do to change things. Work out some ways to make new friends. Make a list of places where you might meet others – at swimming club, at drama group, at gym club. You could ask a parent or teacher to help you.

Tracy's story

The children in Tracy's class were making a painting. They were making it together.

"This way, we can paint a really big picture," said Mrs. Lee, their teacher.

"How will we know which colours to use?" asked Lisa.

"We'll take it in turns to choose a colour," said Mrs Lee.

"I'll go first!" shouted Joseph. "Let's do the sky. Let's paint it blue."

Soon, everyone had a paintbrush dipped in paint. They made a bright, blue sky.

Tracy painted very slowly and carefully. She liked the feeling of the wet brush on the paper. She wanted to go faster, but she was worried that she might go wrong. She was worried that she might spoil the picture.

Every part of the sky had soon been painted. The children washed their brushes to get them clean. Then Mrs Lee asked Hasan to choose a new colour.

"Yellow," he said.

All the children dipped their brushes in yellow paint. Together they painted a huge, yellow sun.

Then it was Lisa's turn. Lisa chose the colour green. After Lisa came Philip. He chose red. Some children splashed the paint. Others dribbled it. But Tracy didn't make one splash or dribble. She was painting very, very slowly.

"It's your turn to choose a colour now, Tracy," said Mrs Lee. All the children looked at Tracy. But Tracy looked down. She didn't say anything. It was very quiet. Everyone was waiting.

Joseph wanted to get on.

"Tracy never knows!" he called. "I know! I know! Let me choose again!"

Mrs Lee wouldn't let Joseph choose again.

"We'll wait for Tracy," she said. But Tracy couldn't think of any colours at all. Everyone was watching her. Tracy felt very small and lonely.

"I'm not like Lisa or Hasan or Joseph. I can't choose a colour. I don't want a turn," thought Tracy.

Have you ever felt like Tracy?

"It's your choice, Tracy," said Mrs Lee again. She sounded kind. Tracy looked at her teacher. She tried to forget about everyone else.

"Purple!" said Tracy at last.

"Purple!" said everyone. "That's just the colour we need!" They all began painting with the thick, purple paint.

Soon the painting was finished. Mrs Lee pinned it up. It stretched all along the wall. Tracy's class was very pleased with the painting.

"Tracy's purple is my favourite colour!" said Joseph. Tracy smiled.

At hometime, everyone rushed towards the door. But Mrs Lee stopped them.

"Hold up your hands, everyone!" she called.

They held their hands above their heads.

"Yes," said Mrs Lee. "You must all wash your hands before you go. They are covered in paint – purple paint." Mrs Lee laughed. "And guess whose are the messiest?"

"Mine!" said Tracy, smiling.

How did Tracy's teacher help?
How do you think Tracy feels now?

Feeling like Tracy

Have you ever felt lonely, like Tracy? Tracy wasn't just shy. She felt that she was different from everyone else. She felt that she couldn't do what the others did. She got used to that feeling.

Being brave

Loneliness is a sad feeling. Sometimes it's easier to be lonely than to join in. But you have to be brave. Think how brave Tracy was when she said "Purple!" It was hard at the time. But it made her feel great afterwards.

You're not alone

It helps to remember that lots of people feel shy and lonely sometimes. You aren't the only one. And you can do something about it. Keep trying. Don't forget to help others, too. If you think that someone else is feeling shy, how could you help them to join in? What would you have done to help Tracy?

Feeling lonely

Think about the stories in this book. Una, Calvin and Tracy all felt lonely. They each found someone to help them. Tell a teacher or a parent how lonely you feel. They'll help you too.

If you are feeling frightened or unhappy, don't keep it to yourself. Talk to an adult you can trust, like a parent or a teacher. If you feel really alone, you could telephone one of these offices. Remember, there is always someone who can help.

ChildLine
Freephone 0800 1111

The Line
ChildLine helpline for young people living away from home
Freephone 0800 884444
3.30pm to 9.30pm (weekdays)
2pm to 8pm (weekends)

NSPCC Child Protection Line
Phone 0808 800 5000

The Samaritans
Phone 08457 909090